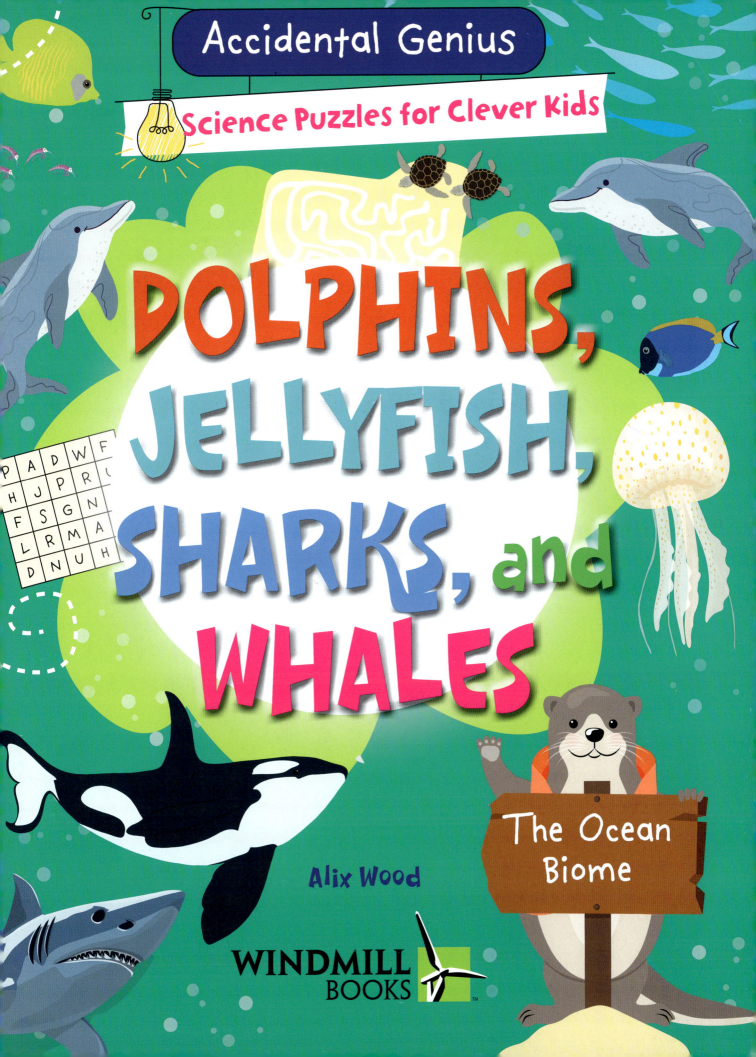

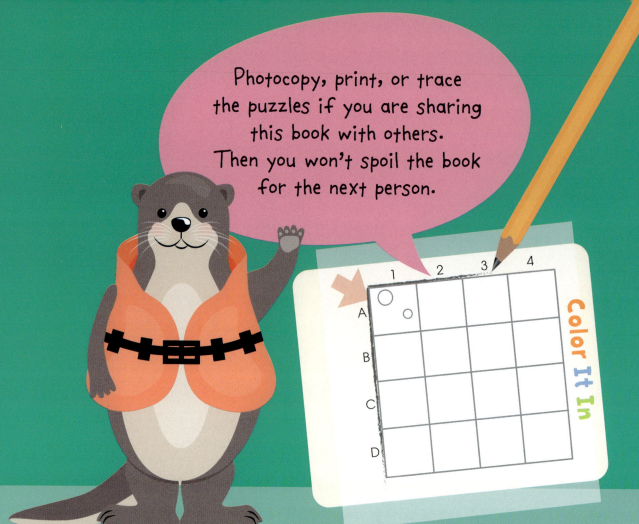

Published in 2024 by Windmill Books,
an Imprint of Rosen Publishing
2544 Clinton Street
Buffalo, NY 14224

Copyright © 2023 Alix Wood Books

Written, designed and illustrated by Alix Wood
All other images © AdobeStock Images

All rights reserved. No part of this book may be reproduced in any form without permission in writing from the publisher, except by a reviewer.

Cataloging-in-Publication Data
Names: Wood, Alix.
Title: Dolphins, jellyfish, sharks, and whales: the ocean biome / Alix Wood.
Description: Buffalo, New York : Windmill Books, 2024. | Series: Accidental genius
Identifiers: ISBN 9781538394786 (pbk.) | ISBN 9781538394793 (library bound) | ISBN 9781538394809 (ebook)
Subjects: LCSH: Marine ecology--Juvenile literature. | Games--Juvenile literature. | Picture puzzles--Juvenile literature.
Classification: LCC QH541.5.S3 W66 2024 | DDC 577.7--dc23

Printed in the United States of America

CPSIA Compliance Information: Batch CSWM24
For Further Information contact Rosen Publishing at 1-800-237-9932

Contents

At Home in the Oceans 4
All Earth's Oceans 6
Ocean Tides 8
Rock Pools 10
River Meets Ocean 12
Near the Surface 14
Coral Reef Homes 16
Ocean Greenery 18
Fantastic Fish 20
Fish Families 22
All About Sharks 24
Ocean Mammals 26
Playful Dolphins 28
Sea Turtles 30
Clever Octopus 32
Jellyfish 34
Ocean Giants 36
Life in the Dark 38
Who Eats Who? 40
Look After the Ocean 42
Ocean Genius Test 44
Answers 46

At Home in the Oceans

Have you ever been to the ocean? Oceans are huge areas of salt water. They cover nearly three-quarters of Earth's surface. Over 90 percent of life on Earth lives in an ocean biome!

What are biomes? Biomes are regions of the world with similar weather and temperature. Each type of biome is home to the plants and animals that can survive in those conditions.

Crabs scuttle sideways along the ocean floor.

Seals speed along underwater using their flippers.

All Earth's Oceans

Although the ocean is actually one big body of water, we split it into five oceans. The oceans are the Atlantic, Pacific, Indian, Arctic, and Southern Oceans.

Copy, print, or trace this picture if you are sharing this book.

Color It In

Color the oceans blue.

Color the land green.

Word Scramble

Can you unscramble these letters and find the names of three oceans? Write your answers on a separate sheet of paper.

1) R I T C A C C _ _ _ _ _ _ _ _ OCEAN

2) N D I I A N _ _ _ _ _ _ _ OCEAN

3) P I C F C A I _ _ _ _ _ _ _ OCEAN

Did You Know?

The Pacific Ocean is the largest and deepest ocean on Earth. It is bigger than all the Earth's land put together!

However, the Pacific is getting 1 inch (2.5 cm) smaller every year. How? Plates that cover Earth's surface are always moving. The Atlantic Ocean is getting bigger by the same amount each year.

Ocean Tides

Tides are the rise and fall of the ocean.
At high tide, the ocean rises up the beach or cliffs.
At low tide, the water pulls away from the land.

Can you tell which of these pictures is high tide and which is low tide?

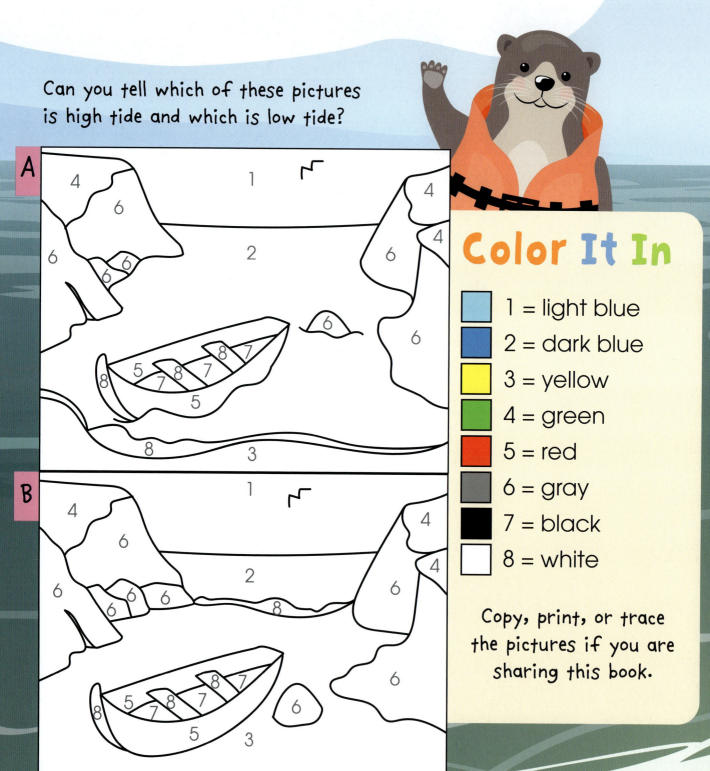

Color It In

- 1 = light blue
- 2 = dark blue
- 3 = yellow
- 4 = green
- 5 = red
- 6 = gray
- 7 = black
- 8 = white

Copy, print, or trace the pictures if you are sharing this book.

Why does the tide go in and out? The moon's gravity pulls at the ocean directly under it, causing a high tide. As that part of Earth spins away from the moon, the tide goes down again.

Gravity is an invisible pulling force. All objects pull things toward their center. Large objects, such as moons and planets, have a strong force of gravity.

As the tide goes out, it leaves a line of debris where the high tide reached. This is called a strandline.

Rock Pools

Waves and tides come in and go out where the ocean meets the land. On rocky coasts, seawater gets trapped in pools between the rocks as the tide goes out. These pools are home to many different underwater creatures.

CRABS
Crabs have eight legs and two claws. They have a hard shell.

STARFISH
Starfish are star-shaped. If they lose an arm, they can grow a new one!

MOLLUSKS
Mollusks have a soft body protected by a hard shell. Clams and sea snails are mollusks.

ANEMONES
Anemones catch prey in their stinging tentacles.

Some creatures live in a rock pool all year round. Others get stuck there by accident when the tide goes out. They are washed back out to sea again when the tide comes in.

If you visit the ocean at low tide, try rockpooling. To stay safe, take an adult, wear sensible shoes, and watch the tide.

Sit so your shadow doesn't fall on the pool. Look in the water. Do you see anything? Look in holes and under ledges. CAREFULLY lift any rocks. There may be a crab hiding underneath. Gently put rocks and creatures back exactly where you found them.

Find these animals in the picture below.

 1 crab    3 sea snails    5 starfish

 2 anemones   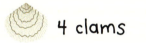 4 clams    6 fish

River Meets Ocean

Ocean water is salty. The area where fresh water from the rivers and salt water from the ocean meet is called an estuary. Animals that live in estuaries have to deal with two different kinds of water!

Why are the oceans salty, but the rivers aren't?

Rain washes mineral salts from the rocks.

Ocean water evaporates, or dries up, into the clouds, but the salts stay behind.

The mineral salts flow into the ocean.

Is Swimming Easier in Salt Water?

You will need: two tall glasses, an egg, warm water, salt

1. Fill two glasses around two-thirds full of warm water. Carefully place an egg into one glass. Record what happens.

2. Add four tablespoons of salt to the second glass of water. Stir well. Place the egg in the water. What happens?

Adding salt makes the water more dense. The first egg sank because it was denser than the water. When enough salt was added, the egg floated. Why? The egg is now lighter than the dense salty water. So, do you think it is easier to swim in salt water or fresh water?

Connect the Dots

Can you see what is hiding in the estuary seagrass? Copy or trace the picture to connect the dots.

Many fish, shellfish, crabs, and marine worms live in estuaries. Leopard sharks go there to give birth to their young. The baby sharks shelter in the seagrass until they are big enough to survive in the ocean.

Near the Surface

The top of the ocean gets the most sunlight. The sunlight provides energy for plants and tiny organisms called plankton. Plants and plankton are very important in the ocean. They are food for a lot of other ocean life.

There are two kinds of plankton: phytoplankton and zooplankton. Phytoplankton are plants. Zooplankton might be eggs, larvae, or newborn sea life such as jellyfish or tiny crabs.

Who eats plankton? Unscramble the scrambled words to find out.

1. GSAULEL
2. BLOSTRE
3. HIFS
4. RCAB

Match each plankton to its partner. Can you find one that doesn't have a match?

Many whales eat zooplankton. They take a mouthful of water. The plankton gets trapped by a filter in their mouth called baleen. The water escapes through the tiny gaps in the baleen.

Coral Reef Homes

Coral is built by tiny animals called coral polyps. The polyps split in half to make new polyps. Eventually, they form a reef. The polyps harden as they die. The rocky reef they form provides food and shelter for hundreds of fish and other sea life.

close-up of a coral polyp

Clown fish choose a strange place to hide from predators: in stinging anemone tentacles! Clown fish are covered in a slime that protects them from the stings.

anemone

clown fish

seahorse

Word Search

Find the eight animals that live in a coral reef. Copy or trace the puzzle if you're sharing this book.

CLOWN FISH
ANEMONE
EEL
CLAM
STARFISH
SEAHORSE
OCTOPUS
JELLYFISH

C	J	E	L	L	Y	F	I	S	H
L	L	P	N	S	G	C	U	L	C
E	S	O	R	N	C	L	R	O	R
O	F	E	W	T	H	A	R	S	S
H	C	P	A	N	E	M	O	N	E
O	S	T	A	R	F	I	S	H	T
R	C	L	O	W	S	I	N	T	S
N	L	I	M	P	P	N	S	G	B
B	E	P	I	N	U	S	U	H	S
S	E	A	H	O	R	S	E	R	S

jellyfish

eel

octopus

clam

starfish

17

Ocean Greenery

Kelp is a type of algae. Kelp provides shelter and food for a lot of sea creatures. Algae is very important for our planet in another way, too. Algae produces oxygen. Oxygen is a gas that people and animals breathe to stay alive.

Do you know how sea otters stick together when they're asleep? They wrap kelp around themselves! The kelp is attached to the seabed, so it acts like an anchor.

Sleeping sea otters sometimes hold hands, too!

All About Kelp

Kelp clings onto the ocean floor using a part called a "holdfast." An air-filled float keeps the kelp upright underwater.

Sea urchins shelter in and eat the tangled holdfasts. Sea otters dive down and eat the sea urchins. Tiny limpets feed on the blades of kelp. Seals and small fish hide from sharks in the forest of fronds.

Did you know we use kelp when we make toothpaste and ice cream?

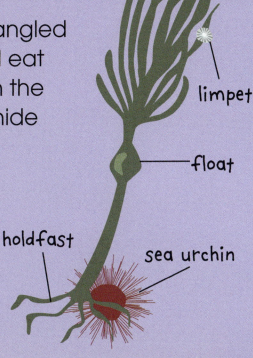

Take the Kelp Quiz!

Test your kelp knowledge! Write your answers on a separate sheet of paper.

1. Kelp is a type of what?
   a) algae   b) fish

2. Finish this sentence: Kelp clings to the ocean floor using its

3. What might hide in a kelp forest?
   a) an elephant   b) a seal

Fantastic Fish

Scientists think around 3.5 trillion fish live in our oceans. That's a lot of fish! Fish live in water. They breathe using special organs called gills. Their bodies are covered in scales. They swim using their fins and tail.

Shadow Match

Fish come in different shapes and sizes. Can you match each fish to their shadow? Write your answers on a separate sheet of paper.

How Do Gills Work?

You will need: two cups, water, a coffee filter, some coffee grounds, a rubber band

1. Secure a coffee filter onto one cup using the rubber band. Make a small dip in the filter to catch the liquid.

2. Fill the other cup halfway with water. Stir in a spoonful of coffee grounds.

3. Carefully pour the liquid through the coffee filter. The filter will catch the grounds. The water will pass through.

Water contains oxygen. When a fish opens its mouth, blood in the gills takes the oxygen from the water. The coffee filter acts like a gill. It collects the coffee grounds (oxygen). The rest of the water filters back into the cup (ocean).

lungs

Animals that don't have gills breathe through lungs. Lungs take oxygen out of the air when the animal breathes in. Then, they breathe out the rest of the gases in the air that the body does not need.

Fish Families

Many types of fish swim in large groups called shoals. Shoals help keep the fish safe. More fish can keep a better lookout for danger. Shoals confuse predators, too. Predators find it hard to pick out a single fish.

Which fish is swimming against the tide?

The Lost Fish

Use your finger to trace the correct path that gets this lost baby fish back to his shoal.

A Fish Family Life Cycle

A life cycle is a series of stages a living thing goes through during its life.

Can you match the pictures to the right stage in the life cycle? We've done the first picture for you. Write your answers on a separate sheet of paper.

A fish starts its life as a tiny egg.

1. SPAWNING
Females lay their eggs in a safe place. The males fertilize them.

2. EGGS
A fish starts to grow inside each egg.

5. ADULT
The fish is fully grown. It can lay or fertilize eggs to start a new life cycle.

?

a

b c

4. JUVENILE
The fish gets bigger but is not quite adult-sized.

d

3. LARVA
The fish hatches. The larva lives off a yolk sac attached to its body.

All About Sharks

Big sharks are the largest predator fish in our oceans. Unlike most fish, they don't have bones. Shark skeletons are made out of cartilage, which bends more easily than bone.

Sharks can sense another animal's heartbeat using special receptors on their heads.

Sharks have several rows of teeth. When a tooth falls out, another one moves forward to replace it.

A shark's sense of smell is 10,000 times better than ours!

Find the Ocean Predator

Copy the drawing in each square into the correct square in the grid below. What did you draw?

Trace the grid onto some paper if you are sharing this book.

We have filled in the first square for you.

Color It In

Ocean Mammals

Not all animals in the ocean are fish. There are mammals that either live or spend most of their time in the water. Whales, seals, walruses, dolphins, manatees, polar bears, and sea otters are all mammals that depend on the oceans.

walrus

polar bear

manatee

seal

sea otter

Mammals feed their young milk. They do not have gills. They come to the surface to breathe.

Word Search

Can you find these 7 mammals? Copy or trace the puzzle if you're sharing this book.

B	E	P	N	A	R	W	H	A	L
L	P	M	O	S	G	B	U	L	M
Z	S	O	K	R	F	X	E	O	A
P	W	E	A	T	P	D	R	S	N
H	A	P	T	N	W	O	L	W	A
E	L	C	R	L	P	L	I	N	T
L	R	L	A	W	S	P	Z	S	E
A	U	E	M	L	P	H	K	G	E
H	S	Y	I	N	G	I	U	C	W
W	L	Q	U	T	V	N	E	B	K

DOLPHIN
WHALE
SEAL
PORPOISE
MANATEE
WALRUS
NARWHAL

porpoise

dolphin

whale

narwhal

27

Playful Dolphins

Dolphins are mammals. They are friendly and love to play. Dolphins are even friendly to humans sometimes. They are also very clever.

Some Clever Things Dolphins Can Do:

1. Recognize themselves in a mirror.

2. Give themselves names. Each dolphin has its own whistle and can say each others' names, too.

3. Dolphins put sea sponges over their beaks. Why? To protect them from sharp rocks as they look for fish!

Dolphins blow bubbles to herd their prey.

Copy or trace the picture if you're sharing this book.

Color It In

A group of dolphins is known as a pod.

Sea Turtles

Large green sea turtles are reptiles. They spend most of their lives in the water. They come to the surface to breathe. When resting, they can last for five hours before they need to come up for air.

A hard shell covers their body.

Their shell can be dark brown, green, or yellow and black.

They move through the water using their four flippers.

Their beak has a jagged edge. It helps them tear food from the rocks.

Green sea turtles eat seagrass and seaweed.

Why are they called green sea turtles if they can be other colors? Because they have a layer of green fat under their shell!

A female sea turtle scuttles onto the beach to lay her eggs. She digs a hole using her flippers. She covers the eggs with sand and heads back to the ocean.

When they hatch, the baby turtles dig their way out of the sand. They wait until dark before they head toward the ocean. The darkness helps hide them from hungry predators.

A Dangerous Journey

Using your finger, trace a path to get these baby turtles safely into the ocean. Don't go near the predators!

Clever Octopus

An octopus is a mollusk. Most mollusks have a hard shell that protects their soft bodies. Octopuses don't have a shell. To hide from predators, they change their skin color and pattern to match the surroundings! They can also squirt an inky liquid that hides them while they escape.

Can you find the 6 hidden octopuses?

Really?

How many of these sentences do you think are true? Write your answers on a separate sheet of paper.

☐ 1. Octopuses can regrow any of their eight long arms.

☐ 2. Octopuses swim backward by blasting water through a tube on their body.

☐ 3. Octopuses have no hard skeleton, so they can squeeze into tiny spaces.

☐ 4. Octopuses have a hard beak.

☐ 5. Octopuses have three hearts.

Connect the Dots

This octopus has lost an arm. Can you help him regrow a new one?

Copy or trace the picture if you are sharing this book with others.

Jellyfish

Jellyfish are strange-looking creatures. Their bag-like bodies can be see-through or brightly colored. Some even glow in the dark!

Jellyfish have no brain, heart, or bones. Most jellyfish have no eyes.

bell or hood

mouth

A jellyfish eats and poops using its mouth! To move, it squirts a jet of water and opens and closes its body like an umbrella.

Jellyfish are not actually fish. Fish have a backbone, and jellyfish don't.

tentacles

Some jellyfish tentacles sting their prey.

Spot the Difference

A group of jellyfish is called a "bloom." Can you find 6 differences between these pictures of a jellyfish bloom?

Ocean Giants

The blue whale is the largest mammal on Earth. It is longer than three buses and heavier than three trucks. Its heart is the size of a small car. Blue whales eat up to 40 million tiny krill a day. Krill are a type of shrimplike zooplankton.

Can you label the parts of the blue whale? The information you need is at the bottom of the page. Write your answers on a separate sheet of paper.

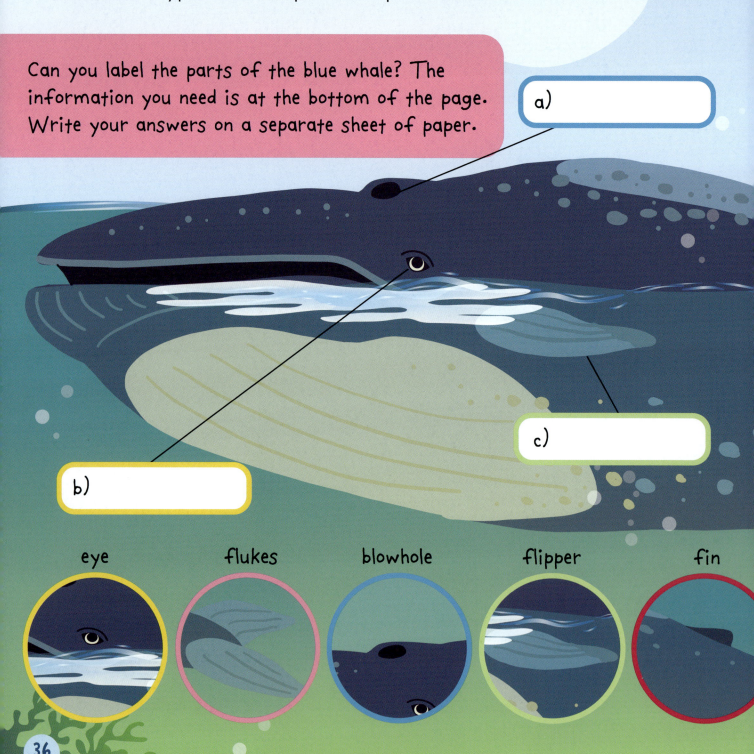

a)
b)
c)

eye   flukes   blowhole   flipper   fin

Draw a Life-Size Blue Whale!

You will need: a tape measure, pebbles, some sidewalk chalk, a large area of sidewalk

1. Measure out 100 feet (30.5 m) along the sidewalk. You may have to use your tape measure several times. Mark the end with a pebble, then measure from that mark. Add the lengths together until you reach 100 feet (30.5 m).

2. Draw a simple outline of a whale. Put an eye one-third of the way down. Draw on the mouth, fluke, and fins.

d)

e)

Blue whales make very loud noises underwater. In calm water, blue whales can hear each other's rumbles and whistles up to 1,000 miles (1,609 km) away!

Life in the Dark

The sun only warms the top of the ocean. Deep down, it is cold and dark. Amazingly, plants still grow. How? They grow around openings in the ocean floor that puff out hot steam! Fish have adapted to live in the dark. Many of them glow or have huge eyes!

The anglerfish has a glowing lure it uses like a fishing rod. The glow attracts small fish into its open mouth.

anglerfish lure

Dead animals fall to the ocean floor. Known as marine snow, their bodies feed many creatures.

hot vent

marine snow

Crossout Puzzle

Copy the grid onto a separate sheet of paper. Cross out any letters that appear twice. Circle each letter that only appears once. Unscramble those letters to find the word to complete this sentence.

The lure of an anglerfish ___ ___ ___ ___ ___.

P	A	D	W	F
H	J	P	R	U
F	S	G	N	M
L	R	M	A	J
D	N	U	H	O

Fish with few or no bones survive best in the deep. The weight of all the water above can crush bones and shells.

worms

jellyfish

squid

Who Eats Who?

Nature provides food for everyone in the ocean. Big fish eat little fish. Little fish eat zooplankton. Large zooplankton eat phytoplankton. Phytoplankton and seaweed get their energy from the sun. This order of who eats who is called a food chain.

The sun gives energy to plankton.

Plankton are food for krill.

Krill are food for fish.

Fish are food for seals.

Orcas are also known as killer whales.

Seals are food for orcas.

Orcas are the top of this food chain. But when they die, their body feeds many other sea creatures.

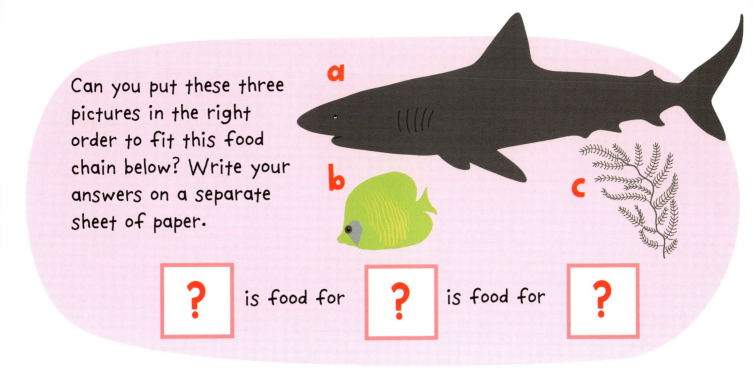

Can you put these three pictures in the right order to fit this food chain below? Write your answers on a separate sheet of paper.

[?] is food for [?] is food for [?]

Animals at the top of their food chain are called apex predators. The orca is an apex predator of the ocean. Using tracing paper, connect the dots to find out what animal is an apex predator of the jungle.

Color It In

Look After the Ocean

We need to look after our oceans. Trash in the ocean harms fish and other sea life. Whales eat tiny beads of plastic, thinking it is krill. Sea turtles eat plastic bags, mistaking them for jellyfish. Seabirds get tangled up in fishing line.

There are plenty of ways to help our ocean friends. You can recycle plastic or stop using it as often. Plastic takes a long time to fall apart. We don't want it in our oceans.

Low Tide Beach Clean

You will need: thick rubber gloves, a trash bag, an adult to help you

Plastic harms animals living in our rivers and oceans. You can help by doing a beach or riverbank clean. As the tide goes out, search the strandline. Put any plastic in a trash bag. Take it home and recycle it. Every piece you pick up may help save an animal's life.

IMPORTANT - Wear gloves, and ask an adult to help you stay safe.

Ocean Genius Test

Are you an ocean biome genius? Answer these questions to find out.

1. Which of these oceans is the largest?

   a) The Arctic Ocean
   b) The Indian Ocean
   c) The Pacific Ocean

2. What causes the tide to go in and out?

   a) the moon and gravity
   b) blue whales flapping their tails
   c) boats

3 Coral is made out of tiny animals. True or false?

a) true   b) false

4 How do fish breathe?

a) using their lungs
b) fish don't breathe
c) using their gills

5 What is a predator?

a) a type of octopus
b) an animal that hunts other animals
c) plankton

Answers

Page 5:

Page 7: 1) Arctic, 2) Indian, 3) Pacific

Page 8: Picture A is high tide; picture B is low tide.

Page 11:

Page 13 top: It is easier to swim in salt water.

Page 13 bottom: A leopard shark is hiding in the seagrass.

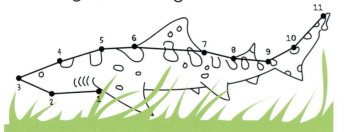

Page 14: 1) seagull, 2) lobster, 3) fish, 4) crab all eat plankton

Page 15:

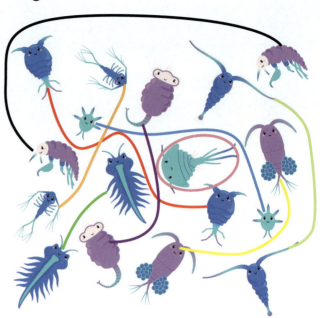

Page 17:

C	J	E	L	L	Y	F	I	S	H
L	L	P	N	S	G	C	U	L	C
E	S	O	R	N	C	L	R	O	R
O	F	E	W	T	H	A	R	S	S
H	C	P	A	N	E	M	O	N	E
O	S	T	A	R	F	I	S	H	T
R	C	L	O	W	S	I	N	T	S
N	L	I	M	P	P	N	S	G	B
B	E	P	I	N	U	S	U	N	S
S	E	A	H	O	R	S	E	R	S

Page 19: 1) a - Kelp is a type of algae. 2) Kelp clings to the ocean floor using its holdfast. 3) b - A seal might hide in a kelp forest.

46

Page 20: 1) c, 2) a, 3) b

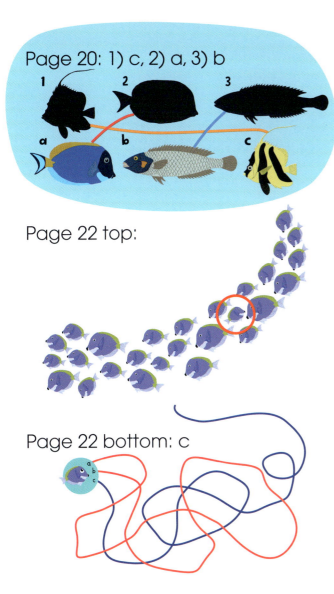

Page 22 top:

Page 22 bottom: c

Page 23: 2) b, 3) c, 4) d, 5) a

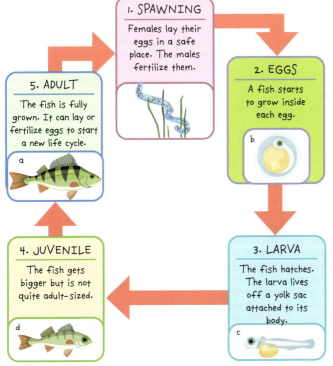

Page 25: a shark

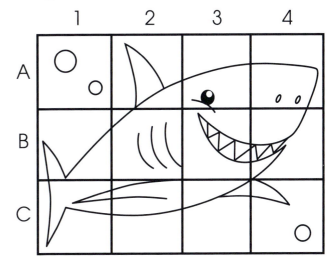

Page 27:

Page 31:

47

Page 32:

Page 33 top: Facts 1-5 are all true.

Page 33 bottom:

Page 35:

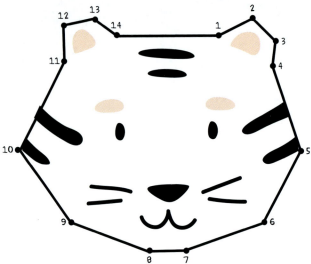

Page 37: a) blowhole, b) eye, c) flipper, d) fin, e) flukes

Page 39: An anglerfish lure GLOWS.

Page 41 top: C (a plant) is food for b (a fish) is food for a (a shark).

Page 41 bottom: An apex predator of the jungle is a tiger.

Page 44: 1) c - The Pacific Ocean is the largest. 2) a - The moon and gravity cause the tides to go in and out. 3) a - True, coral is made out of tiny animals. 4) c - Fish breathe using their gills. 5) b - A predator is an animal that hunts other animals.